**Steve Blount, Peter Daly,
Gavin Kostick and Janet Moran**

Swing

T0353330

Bloomsbury Methuen Drama
An imprint of Bloomsbury Publishing Plc

B L O O M S B U R Y
LONDON · OXFORD · NEW YORK · NEW DELHI · SYDNEY

Bloomsbury Methuen Drama

An imprint of Bloomsbury Publishing Plc

Imprint previously known as Methuen Drama

50 Bedford Square	1385 Broadway
London	New York
WC1B 3DP	NY 10018
UK	USA

www.bloomsbury.com

Bloomsbury is a registered trade mark of Bloomsbury Publishing Plc

First published 2016

British Library Cataloguing-in-Publication Data
A catalogue record for this book is available from the British Library.

ISBN: PB: 978-1-3500-0222-7
ePub: 978-1-3500-0221-0
ePDF: 978-1-3500-0223-4

Library of Congress Cataloging-in-Publication Data
A catalog record for this book is available from the Library of Congress.

Typeset by Mark Heslington Ltd, Scarborough, North Yorkshire

fishamble
THE NEW PLAY COMPANY

presents

Swing

by

Steve Blount, Peter Daly, Gavin Kostick and Janet Moran

**On tour in Ireland, the UK and Australia
March–June 2016**

Joe/Teacher 1/ George/Rough Guy/Sean/Justin/Geeky Guy/
Uncomprehending Guy/Stinky Guy/Robert/Gerald
Arthur Riordan

May/Teacher 2/Sally/Terrified Girl/Regina/
Imelda/Noelia/Choking Girl/Julia
Gene Rooney

Director	Peter Daly
Producer	Eva Scanlan
Lighting Designer	Mark Galione
Sound Designer	Ivan Birthistle
Artistic Director, Fishamble	Jim Culleton
Stage Manager	Marella Boschi

RUNNING TIME: 60 minutes

Swing was developed as part of **Show in a Bag**,
an artist development initiative of Dublin Fringe Festival,
Fishamble: The New Play Company and Irish Theatre Institute
to resource theatre makers and actors. It premiered at Dublin
Fringe Festival in 2013, and has been produced since then by
Fishamble on tour in Ireland, UK, France, US, New Zealand
and Australia. From 2013 to 2015, all the roles were performed
by Janet Moran and Steve Blount, who also co-wrote the play.

Steve Blount – Writer

Steve's previous acting work for Fishamble includes *Tiny Plays for Ireland 1*, *Tiny Plays for Ireland 2*, *Pilgrims in the Park* and *Swing*. Other theatre includes *A Streetcar Named Desire* (Gate Theatre), *Across the Lough* (Performance Corporation), *Paisley and Me* (Belfast Opera House and NI tour), *Bog Boy* (Tall Tales and Irish Arts Center, New York), *Only and Apple*, *Savoy*, *The Wild Duck*, *Judas of the Gallarus*, *The Pauper*, *She Stoops to Folly* (Abbey Theatre), *Tarry Flynn* (Abbey Theatre/National Theatre, London), *I Swapped My Dad for Two Goldfish* (The Ark), *The Temple of Clown* (Barabbas), *The Night Garden*, *All My Sons* (Northcott Theatre, Exeter), *No Place Like Home* (Tinderbox), *The Seagull* (Corn Exchange), *Romeo and Juliet* (Pavilion), *Oedipus* (Gaiety), *A Whistle in the Dark* (Lyric Theatre), *Melody* (Tall Tales), *The Sin Eaters* (New Balance Dance), *Accidental Death of an Anarchist* (Blue Raincoat), *Submarine* (Bewleys), *One*, *Martin Assassin of His Wife* (Pan Pan), *Waiting for Lefty* (65th Street Theater, Seattle), *Blithe Spirit* (Theatre Factory, Texas). Film and television work includes *Moone Boy*, *Titanic*, *Blood and Steel*, *Game of Thrones*, *The Race*, *32A*, *Single Handed*, *Prosperity*, *The Clinic*, *Stolen Child*, *Stardust*, *Breakfast on Pluto*, *Bachelors Walk*, *Fair City*, *Glenroe*, *The Colleen Bawn*, *Agnes Browne*, *Mad About Mambo*, *Pips*, *Johnny Loves Suzy* and *Though the Sky*.

Peter Daly – Writer and Director

Peter's previous acting work for Fishamble includes *Guaranteed!*, *Tiny Plays for Ireland 1*, *Tiny Plays for Ireland 2* and *Bailed Out!* Other recent acting work includes *DruidShakespeare* (Druid), *The Critic*, *Jezebel*, *Travesties*, *Peer Gynt*, *The Importance of Being Earnest*, *Life Is a Dream*, *Don Carlos*, *Attempts on Her Life*, *The Taming of the Shrew* (Rough Magic), *The Government Inspector*, *Arrah Na Pogue*, *The Comedy of Errors*, *The Shaughraun*, *The Cherry Orchard* (Abbey Theatre), *Death of a Salesman* (Gate Theatre), *The Dead School* & *Conversations on a Homecoming* (Livin Dred). Film and television work includes *Trivia*, *The Mario Rosenstock Show*, *Fair City*, *The Clinic*, and *Love Is the Drug* (RTÉ). Radio includes *The Eamon Lowe Show* (Today FM).

Gavin Kostick – Writer

As Literary Manager at Fishamble: The New Play Company, Gavin works with new writers for theatre through script development for production, readings and a variety of mentorship programmes such as *Show in a Bag* and *The New Play Clinic*. Gavin is also an award-winning playwright. He has written over a twenty plays which have been produced in Dublin, and on tour around Ireland, the UK, New York. Recent works include *The End of the Road* for Fishamble, *This is What We Sang* for Kabosh (Belfast and New York), *An Image for the Rose*, *Trilogy* outdoors for Whiplash Theatre Company and *Fight Night*, *The Games People Play* and *At the Ford* for RISE Productions. *The Games People Play* received the Irish Times Award for best new play. He wrote the libretto for *The Alma Fetish*, composed by Raymond Deane, which was staged in 2014 by WideOpenOpera at the National Concert Hall. As a performer he performed *Joseph Conrad's Heart of Darkness: Complete*, a six-hour show for Dublin Fringe, Dublin Theatre Festival and the London Festival of Literature at the Southbank.

Janet Moran – Writer

Janet's previous acting work for Fishamble includes *Spinning* and *Swing*. Other stage work includes *Juno and the Paycock* (National Theatre, London/Abbey Theatre co-production), *Shibari*, *Translations, No Romance, The Recruiting Officer, The Cherry Orchard, She Stoops to Conquer, Communion, The Barbaric Comedies, The Well of the Saints, The Hostage* (Abbey Theatre), *The Bridge Below the Town* (Livin' Dred Theatre Company), *Car Show, Dublin by Lamplight, Everyday, Freefall, Desire Under the Elms (*Corn Exchange), *Dead Funny* (Rough Magic), *Stella by Starlight* (Gate Theatre), *Romeo and Juliet, Othello* (Second Age). Other theatre includes *Pineapple, Xaviers, Royal Supreme, Her Big Chance, Unravelling the Ribbon, Dancing at Lughnasa, Playing from the Heart, Guess Who's Coming for the Dinner, All's Well That Ends Well, The Rep Experiment, The Stomping Ground.* Film and television work includes *Bridget & Eamon, Trivia, Love/Hate, Love is the Drug, The Clinic* (RTE), *The Butcher Boy, Breakfast on Pluto, Milo, Minim Rest, Bono and My Ex, Moll Flanders, Nothing Personal, Volkswagen Joe* and *Quirke* (BBC).

Arthur Riordan – Actor

Arthur has previously performed in Fishamble's production of *Wired to the Moon*. He is a founder member of Rough Magic and has appeared in many of their productions, including *Peer Gynt, Improbable Frequency, Solemn Mass for a Full Moon in Summer*, and more. He has also worked with the Abbey and Peacock Theatres, Gaiety Theatre, Corcadorca, Pan Pan, Druid, the Corn Exchange, Bedrock Productions, Red Kettle, Project, Bewleys Café Theatre and most recently, with Livin' Dred, in their production of *The Kings of the Kilburn High Road.* Film and TV appearances include *Out of Here, Ripper Street, The Clinic, Fair City, Refuge, Borstal Boy, Rat, Pitch 'n' Putt* with *Joyce'n'Beckett, My Dinner with Oswald.*

Arthur has also written several plays including *The Train, Improbable Frequency, Peer Gynt* (a new adaptation) and *The Emergency Session,* all for Rough Magic; *Slattery's Sago Saga* (adapted from the unfinished Flann O'Brien novel) for the Performance Corporation; *Shooting Gallery* (co-written with Des Bishop) for Bedrock Productions; *Rap Eire,* (also with Des Bishop (for Bickerstaffe)); and *Love Me?!* for the Corn Exchange.

Gene Rooney – Actor

Gene is a proud Limerick woman. This is her debut with Fishamble. She is a graduate of the Gaiety School of Acting. Since then she has performed on almost every stage in Ireland in over forty productions. Some favourites include: *Buck Jones and the Bodysnatchers* (Joan Sheehy Productions and Dublin Theatre Festival), *The Colleen Bawn Trials* (Limerick City of Culture), *Pigtown, The Taming of the Shrew, Lovers* (Island Theatre Company*), Excess Baggage* (The Hub, Limerick), *The Revengers Tragedy* (Bottom Dog), *The Importance of Being Earnest* (Gúna Nua), *Our Father* (With an F Productions), *How I Learned to Drive* (Lyric Theatre, Belfast), *I ♥ Alice ♥ I* (Hot for Theatre), *Do Not Adjust Yourself* (Pinfish), *St Agúna's* (Read Co), *Crabbed Youth and Age* (Bewley's), and most recently *The 24 Hour Plays* (Abbey Theatre). TV and film work includes *Moone Boy, Stella Days, The Sea, Hideaways, Killinaskully, Botched, The Last Furlong* and *The Clinic.* Radio includes *Excess Baggage, Ghost Bike* and *After the Fact* (all RTE radio). Gene teaches acting and improvisation at the Gaiety School of Acting – the National Theatre School of Ireland and directed their graduation showcase for twelve years. She also teaches improvisation at the Irish Film Academy.

Eva Scanlan – Producer

In 2016, Eva returned to Fishamble: The New Play Company as General Manager and Producer. Previously, she was Producer of terraNOVA Collective in New York (2012–2015), where she produced *terraNOVA Rx: Four Plays in Rep* at IRT Theater, the soloNOVA Arts Festival, the Groundworks New Play Series, *Woman of Leisure and Panic* (FringeNYC), *P.S. Jones and the Frozen City,* among other projects.

Eva produces *The 24 Hour Plays: Dublin* at the Abbey Theatre in Ireland (2012–2016), in association with the 24 Hour Play Company, New York, and she has worked on *The 24 Hour Plays* on Broadway and *The 24 Hour Musicals* at the Gramercy Theatre. Recent work includes producing *At the Ford* for Rise Productions, written by Gavin Kostick and directed by Bryan Burroughs, and as line producer for *I'm Your Man* by Mark Matthew Palmer and Phillip McMahon for Project Arts Centre and ThisIsPopBaby, both as part of the Dublin Theatre Festival 2016. Previous work for Fishamble includes *Silent* (Irish tour), *Forgotten* (Irish tour, New York, Boston, Washington, DC, Bulgaria, Turkey, Iceland), *The Pride of Parnell Street* (2011 Irish tour, 2009 New York), *Noah and the Tower Flower* (New York), *Big Ol' Piece of Cake* and *Strandline*, and she has worked as production coordinator of *Macbeth* for Second Age Theatre Company (Irish tour).

Previous arts administration work includes the Arts Council of Ireland and the Corn Exchange Theatre Company. Eva has an MA in Film Production and PgDip in Business in Cultural Event Management.

Mark Galione – Lighting Designer
Mark's designs in Ireland include works for Fishamble: The New Play Company, Irish Modern Dance Theatre, Cois Ceim, Dance Theatre of Ireland, The Peacock, Fíbín, Hands Turn, Classic Stage Ireland, Barabbas, Vesuvius, The Derry Playhouse, The Ark, Peer to Peer, Gonzo, Theatre Lovett, Second Age and Barnstorm. In the UK his lighting designs included work for Nigel Charnock, Emilyn Claid, Ricochet, Small Axe, Gaby Agis, Sadler's Wells, the Royal Ballet, Sherman Theatre and Soho Theatre Company. Recent TV includes *Jack Lukeman 27 Club, All Ireland Schools Talent Search* (TG4*) Country Music Legends, The Al Porter Christmas Show* (RTE2).

Ivan Birthistle – Sound Designer
Ivan mostly works with Vincent Doherty on an ongoing collaborative basis. Ivan is head of the Sound Department and resident sound designer at the Lir National Academy of Dramatic Arts. He has been working as a composer and sound designer in theatre for fifteen years and has worked with nearly every major theatre company in the country. He has also played in many bands over the years notably *Schtum* and *Nina Hynes and the Husbands*, and has released several records.

Past work for Fishamble includes *Swing, The Great Goat Bubble, Tiny Plays For Ireland 1, Tiny Plays for Ireland 2, The End of the Road, Rank, Noah and the Tower Flower, Monged* (Fishamble). Other work includes *The Motherfucker with the Hat* (Orion Productions); *Dublin OldSchool* (Project Arts Centre), *The Wolf and Peter, Agnes, Pageant, Touch Me* (CoisCeim), *The White Piece* (IMDT), *Re-energize, Over The Wire* (Derry Playhouse), *Monsters Dinosaurs Ghosts, The Picture Of Dorian Gray, No Escape, Playboy of the Western World, Saved, Alice Trilogy, True West* (Abbey Theatre), *Dockers, The Absence of Women, The Beauty Queen of Leenane, Homeplace, Dancing at Lughnasa, True West* (Lyric Theatre, Belfast), *The Field* (Lane Productions), *The Boys Of Foley Street, Laundry* (ANU Productions), *Freefall* (The Corn Exchange), *All in the Timing* (Innis Theatre Co.), *The Sanctuary Lamp* (B'spoke), *Dying City, Pentecost* (Rough Magic), *This Is Our Youth, Wedding Day at the Cro-Magnons', Roberto Zucco* (Bedrock), *Ladies and Gents, God's Grace, Adrenalin* and *Slaughter* (Semper-Fi).

Jim Culleton – Artistic Director
Jim is Artistic Director of Fishamble: The New Play Company for which he has directed award-winning productions that have toured throughout Ireland, UK, US, Canada, Australia and twelve European countries. He has also directed for the Abbey Theatre, and many other companies in Ireland and elsewhere.

Marella Boschi – Stage Manager
Marella arrived in Ireland from Italy in 1993. After graduating in the Inchicore VEC College, Stagecraft course, she has been employed full time in theatre, mostly in stage management; but also operating sound and lights, and occasionally designing costumes and sets, with the opportunity to work in most theatres in Dublin, to tour Ireland many times, and to travel to New York, London, Edinburgh, Paris, Belgium, and Poland, with different shows. Being freelance, she has had the pleasure to work for many companies, including Fishamble: The New Play Company, the Abbey Theatre, Second Age, Axis Productions, Gúna Nua, Calypso, Common Currency, Opera Ireland, Wexford Opera Festival, and Ulysses Opera Theatre. In 2001 she toured Ireland as stage director for a monologue she had translated from Italian into English, *1900 The Pianist on the Ocean*, produced by the Civic Theatre.

About Fishamble: The New Play Company

Fishamble is an award-winning, internationally acclaimed Irish theatre company, dedicated to the discovery, development and production of new work. Fishamble is committed to touring in Dublin, throughout Ireland and internationally, and typically presents over 200 performances of its plays in approximately 60 venues per year.

Fishamble has earned a reputation as 'a global brand with international theatrical presence' (*Irish Times*), 'forward-thinking Fishamble' (*New York Times*), 'acclaimed Irish company' (*Scotsman*) and 'excellent Fishamble . . . Ireland's terrific Fishamble' (*Guardian*) through touring its productions to audiences in Ireland as well as to England, Scotland, Wales, France, Germany, Iceland, Croatia, Belgium, Czech Republic, Switzerland, Bulgaria, Romania, Serbia, Turkey, Finland, USA, Canada, New Zealand and Australia.

Awards for Fishamble productions include Scotsman Fringe First, Herald Angel, Argus Angel, MAMCA, 1st Irish, The Stage, Adelaide Fringe Best Theatre and Irish Times Theatre Awards, as well as Stewart Parker Trust Awards for many of its first-time playwrights, and nominations for EMA, Business to Arts, Total Theatre and Olivier Awards. During 2013, to celebrate the company's 25th birthday, Fishamble donated its living archive to the National Library of Ireland.

Fishamble is at the heart of new writing for theatre in Ireland, not just through its productions, but through its extensive programme of Training, Development and Mentoring schemes. Each year, Fishamble typically supports 60% of the writers of all new plays produced on the island of Ireland, approximately 55 plays per year. This happens in a variety of ways; for instance, Fishamble supports:

➤ **the public** through an ongoing range of playwriting courses in Dublin and off-site for venues and festivals nationwide

➤ **playwrights and theatre companies** through *The New Play Clinic*, which develops new plays planned for production by theatre artists and companies, and the annual *Fishamble New Writing Award* at Dublin Fringe

➤ **actors** through its *Show in a Bag* programme, which creates and showcases new plays for actors, in association with the Irish Theatre Institute and Dublin Fringe Festival

➤ **students** through work in association with TCD, NUIG, NUIM, IES, DIT, GSA, Uversity and as *Theatre Company in Association* at UCD

➤ **emerging artists** through *Mentoring Schemes* in association with venues and local authorities, for playwrights and directors.

'Ireland's terrific Fishamble' ***Guardian*, 2015**

'Fishamble puts electricity in the National grid of dreams'
Sebastian Barry

fishamble.com   facebook.com/fishamble   twitter.com/fishamble

Fishamble's World Premiere Productions

Recent and current productions include:

- *Inside the GPO* by Colin Murphy (2016) performed in the GPO for Easter 2016
- *Tiny Plays for Ireland and America* by 26 writers (2016) at the Kennedy Center, Washington DC, and Irish Arts Center, New York, as part of *Ireland 100*
- *Eileen Gray – Invitation to a Journey* by David Bolger, Deirdre Gribbin and Gavin Kostick (2016) in coproduction with CoisCeim, Crash Ensemble and Galway International Arts Festival
- *Underneath* by Pat Kinevane (2014–16) winner of The Scotsman Fringe First Award, Adelaide Fringe Best Theatre Award, touring in Ireland, UK, Europe, US, Australia
- *Little Thing, Big Thing* by Donal O'Kelly (2014–16) winner of The Stage Award for Acting Excellence and 1st Irish Best Production Award, touring in Ireland, UK, Europe, New York, Australia
- *Silent* by Pat Kinevane (2011–2016) winner of The Scotsman Fringe First Award, Herald Angel Award, Argus Angel Award, nominated for an Olivier Award, touring in Ireland, UK, Europe, US, Australia
- *Swing* by Steve Blount, Peter Daly, Gavin Kostick and Janet Moran (2014–16) touring in Ireland, UK, Europe, US, Australia and New Zealand
- *Forgotten* by Pat Kinevane (2007–16) touring in Ireland, UK, Europe, US
- *Spinning* by Deirdre Kinahan (2014) at Dublin Theatre Festival

- *The Wheelchair on My Face* by Sonya Kelly (2013–14) winner of The Scotsman Fringe First Award, touring in Ireland, UK, Europe, US

Fishamble has produced plays written by:

Sebastian Barry, Maeve Binchy, Sarah Binchy*, Steve Blount*, Dermot Bolger, Dawn Bradfield*, Mark Cantan, Marina Carr, Shane Carr*, Michael Collins, John Austin Connolly, Ciara Considine*, Niamh Creely*, John Cronin*, Michael Cussen, Tara Dairman*, Evan Lee D'Alton*, Peter Daly*, Steve Daunt*, Bryan Delaney*, Talaya Delaney*, Darren Donohoe, Gary Duggan*, Aino Dubrawsky*, Keith Farnan*, Stella Feehily*, Rachel Fehily*, Mike Finn, Ronan Geoghegan*, Kevin Gildea*, Ger Gleeson*, Julian Gough*, Brendan Griffin*, John Grogan*, Conor Hanratty*, Antonia Hart*, Rosalind Haslett*, James Heaney*, Mark Hennessy*, Deirdre Hines*, Róisín Ingle*, Jennifer Johnston, Nicholas Kelly*, Sonya Kelly*, Stephen Kennedy, Garrett Keogh, Marian Keyes*, Ian Kilroy*, Deirdre Kinahan, Pat Kinevane*, Gavin Kostick*, Rodney Lee*, Adrienne Michel Long*, Louise Lowe, Colm Maher*, Henry Martin*, Robert Massey*, Geraldine McAlinden*, Lorraine McArdle*, Colum McCann*, Belinda McKeon*, Christine McKeon*, Rosaleen McDonagh, Pauline McLynn*, Justine Mitchell*, Lucy Montague-Moffatt*, Janet Moran*, Gina Moxley, Colin Murphy*, Gerald Murphy, Anna Newell*, Ciara Ni Chuirc*, Rory Nolan*, Joseph O'Connor*, Simon O'Gorman*, Ardal O'Hanlon*, Jim O'Hanlon*, Donal O'Kelly, Jack Olohan*, Jody O'Neill*, Karl O'Neill, Mark O'Rowe*, Patrick O'Sullivan*, Richie O'Sullivan*, Mary Portser, Liz Quinn*, Michelle Read*, Tina Reilly*, Gregory Rosenstock, Joan Ryan*, Abbie Spallen, Federico Storni*, Jacqueline Strawbridge*, Graham Stull*, Sean P. Summers*, Tom Swift, Colin Teevan, Jesse Weaver, Michael West, Eleanor White*, Tanya Wilson*.

* denotes first play by a new playwright as part of *Fishamble Firsts*

New plays are under commission from:

Sebastian Barry, Gavin Kostick, Deirdre Kinahan, Pat Kinevane, Darren Donohue, Colin Murphy and Rosaleen McDonagh.

Fishamble Staff: Jim Culleton (Artistic Director), Eva Scanlan (General Manager), Gavin Kostick (Literary Manager)

Fishamble Needs Your Support

Become a **Friend of Fishamble** today and support new theatre making at its best, while enjoying the benefits of complimentary tickets, discounts on playwriting courses and more!

Please contact Eva Scanlan for further details on 00 353 670 4018 or *eva@fishamble.com*

Fishamble is funded by the Arts Council and Dublin City Council. Its international touring is supported by Culture Ireland.

Comhairle Cathrach
Bhaile Átha Cliath
Dublin City Council

ARTISTIC DIRECTOR'S NOTE

In 2010, the Dublin Fringe Festival, Irish Theatre Institute and Fishamble wanted to create an initiative that would support theatre artists to make easily tourable work, helping actors to have their own 'show in a bag', and offer venues throughout Ireland the chance to programme top-quality work that has been developed with the support of the three organisations. *Show in a Bag (SIAB)* has helped to create twenty-eight shows so far, with many of them – including *Swing, The Wheelchair on My Face, Beowulf: The Blockbuster, Fight Night, Charolais, Dublin Oldschool* and *Small Plastic Wars* – touring throughout Ireland and internationally, winning major awards at the Edinburgh Fringe and elsewhere.

One of the joys of *SIAB* is that it encourages and supports actors to consider, often for the first time, creating a show for themselves to perform. So when Janet Moran and Steve Blount, two of Ireland's most respected actors, applied to create a show about a couple who meet at Swing dance classes, we were thrilled to help them create the show. Fishamble's Literary Manager, Gavin Kostick, works with the actors as dramaturg on all the *SIAB* plays, sometimes writing or co-writing them. He worked with Janet and Steve to co-write the play, and they were joined by Peter Daly, who also directed the production, as the fourth member of the writing team. It has been a pleasure working with them, right from the start. Together, they have created a beautiful and uplifting play, full of humanity and insight. Audiences have responded so positively to the play as it has such an enjoyably wicked sense of humour but also has a lot to say, in its unassuming way, about the power we have to help each other through life's challenges.

Fishamble is very grateful to all our partners who have worked with us on the *Swing* tour, including many Irish theatres and arts centres, the Irish Arts Center (New York), Centre Culturel Irlandais (Paris), Dance Base (Edinburgh), and Christchurch Arts Festival and Auckland Live (New Zealand). The revival in 2016 is happening in partnership with Irish venues, House in the UK and Merrigong Theatre Company in Australia, and we are very grateful to them for making it happen. Thanks also to our *SIAB* partners at Dublin Fringe

Festival and the Irish Theatre Institute, to the Arts Council and Dublin City Council, both of which support Fishamble to create new work for theatre in a range of ways, and Culture Ireland, without which none of the international touring would happen.

Jim Culleton, 2016

GLOSSARY

Amazebeams, amazebums, amazeballs, amazingtons, amazoids, amazalicious! = amazing.

Bloom = Bloom Festival. Ireland's largest gardening show.

Bohs = Bohemian Football Club. Another professional football club from Dublin and rivals to the Hoops.

Botanic Gardens = the National Botanic Gardens. Located in Glasnevin, Dublin. Founded in 1795, it is Ireland's second most visited free attraction.

Ceili = Ceili dances. A popular form of folk dancing in Ireland.

Crips = chips.

Dragon = a gay bar in Dublin which does not run a bingo night on a Sunday night.

Dzope(s) = dope(s) = fool(s).

Fillums = films.

Gaeltacht = an Irish-speaking region.

George = a gay bar in Dublin which runs a bingo night on a Sunday night.

Hoops = Hoops Rovers = Shamrock Rovers Football Club. A professional football club from Dublin.

J-1 = a non-immigrant visa issued by the United States to exchange visitors participating in programmes that promote cultural exchange.

Joe Duffy – an Irish broadcaster employed by Raidió Teilifís Éireann (RTÉ). One of RTÉ's highest earning stars, he is the current presenter of Liveline, which is broadcast on RTÉ Radio 1.

Kerry = a county in the south west of Ireland.

Kip = dump (slang), e.g. 'The city was a complete kip'.

Leaving = the leaving certificate, the final examination in the Irish secondary school system.

Mocks = practice exams taken a few months before the leaving certificate to prepare students for exam conditions.

Pantibar = a gay bar in Dublin run by Miss Panti, an institution of the gay community in Ireland who is widely considered to be Dublin's foremost drag queen.

Parnell Mooney = a bar in Dublin. Now called the Parnell Heritage Pub & Grill. Named after Charles Stewart Parnell who was an Irish landlord, nationalist political leader, land-reform agitator, and the founder and leader of the Irish Parliamentary Party.

Port Tunnel = a road traffic tunnel in Dublin. It is the third-longest urban motorway tunnel in Europe.

Ronan = Ronan Keating, an Irish recording artist, singer-songwriter, musician and philanthropist.

Yoke = thing.

Swing

Characters

May
Joe
Teacher 1 *and* **Teacher 2** *are married to each other . . . but also may hate each other. They have a veneer of professional friendliness but always take the opportunity to take a swipe at each other. He thinks he is hilarious (he is not, he is cheesy) and she has the propensity to snap at people in the class, especially if they are not paying attention to her.*
Sally *and* **George** *are older and from Dublin. They come every week and are good dancers. George, a bit of a bull in a china shop, is in love with Sally and constantly asks her out but she prefers 'to fly solo'. She may have a distinctive laugh.*
Rough Guy
Terrified Girl
Sean, *who is rural, can't really dance and takes big awkward steps but is trying very hard.*
Regina, *from Northern Ireland, who is stuck-up, is very good dancer but knows it and is cruel about people who can't dance.*
Justin *is very flamboyant and interested in gossip.*
Imelda *is from Cork, youngish and has absolutely no filter.*
Geeky Guy
Noelia *is from Spain.*
Uncomprehending Guy
Stinky Guy
Choking Girl
Robert
Gerald and Julia

The stage is empty apart from two chairs, one stage left and one stage right.

Act One

Scene One

The first pre-class

May *enters the same way that the audience has entered. She regards the audience as if they are also people who are here for a swing dance class.*

May   Swing?

Swing?

Sorry, is this swing?

She usually gets a response in the affirmative at this stage.

She is satisfied that she is in the right place. But she is unsure where to place herself.

She spots the chairs and goes to the stage-right chair. She remembers her jacket and takes it off to reveal a fifties-style swing dress. She looks down at it and then at the audience.

I'm a bit overdressed.

She stretches and in doing so smells under her oxters. She may be a bit sweaty. She takes out deodorant, starts to apply it, spots someone in the audience looking at her, turns around and continues to apply it, and then puts it back in the bag.

She checks her breath to see if it is fresh. It may not be. She asks an audience member:

Do you have any chewing gum?

Before they have a chance to answer she says:

Oh wait! I think I have some!

She gets some chewing gum from her bag, takes it from the wrapper, chews it, puts it in a tissue she finds in her bag and drops this in her bag. She looks around again.

She adjusts her knickers and bra. As she is picking the knickers out of her bum, with her back to the audience –

Joe *enters, also from the audience. He is wearing bicycle gear including a flashing light on his bicycle helmet. He sees the audience.*

Joe   Swing?

Swing?

*The audience usually give him a big yes at this stage as they recognise this from **May** asking them the same thing.*

Joe (*indicating some audience members*)   Thought it might have been hip hop!

*He spots the other chair and goes to it. He doesn't see **May**.*

As he takes off his gear and gets his water and towel ready, he addresses members of the audience as if they are people he has met in the class before. These are some possible ad-libs:

– Ah you came back! Good on ya! Very brave! . . . Considering . . .

– Ah howya, how's the foot? Listen sorry about last week . . .

He starts to hum and then breaks into the lyrics of 'It don't mean a thing, if it ain't got that.'

*Just before he gets to the 'Swing' in the song, he spots **May**. She is stretching her leg.*

This silences him. He may look at the audience.

She is not looking at him at first.

He copies her stretch.

She spots him doing so. This stops her as she is now a little self-conscious.

She looks over at him again.

He smiles a big broad smile.

She looks away – she is unsure if he is looking at her.

She looks back and gives him a tentative smile.

She spots his bicycle clip, which he has forgotten to take off.

She nods at it.

He does a big nod back.

She nods again – bigger – and indicates the clips.

When he cops this he takes it off.

Joe (*mouthing*)   You're new.

May (*normal voice*)   Sorry?

Joe (*mouthing*)   You're new.

May   I'm who?

Joe (*quite loud*)   You're new!

May   Oh, yes.

Joe   You're very welcome.

He then walks towards her, hand out to shake hers.

My name is /

As they touch hands they transform into the **Teachers**. *Usually when we see the* **Teachers** *for the first time they shoot their arms up in the air – imagine someone who is giving a class getting everyone's attention at the start.*

Scene Two

The first Teachers' scene

Teacher 2 (*female, English*)   Ok, everyone, we're going to get started!

Teacher 1 (*male*)   It's our first week back. Are we ready to work off those summer pints and picnics /

Teacher 2   / and ice-creams /

Teacher 1   / I see some old faces /

Teacher 2   / we've really missed you!

Teacher 1   and some new.

Teacher 2 (*shrill and much to* **Teacher 1***'s annoyance*)   Yaay!

Teacher 1   Anyone here *never* been swing dancing before?

Teacher 2   Ok great, lots of new faces.

Teacher 1   Don't worry if you don't have a partner. We're swingers, so everyone gets to change partner a lot.

Teacher 2   That joke's getting a bit old.

Teacher 1 (*snaps*)   Never gets old!

Beat.

Teacher 2   Ok, let's do the basic rock step.

Teacher 1   This is East Coast swing, so it's a six count. Look up here –

'Leads' (*Indicating himself.*) back on the left, 'follows' (*Indicating* **Teacher 2**.) back on the right.

And it's . . . rock step, triple step, triple step . . . That's . . . rock step, triple step, triple step. Got that?

Teacher 2   Yaay! Let's give it a go! Annnnd . . .

Both   Rock step, triple and your triple. And your rock step, triple and your triple.

Teacher 1   Ok, everyone, find a partner and let's try each other out for size!

Teacher 2   We'll practise the step without music so you can go at your own pace. Ok? Aaaannnnndd 5/6/7/8 . . .

As **Teacher 2** *says '5/6/7/8' they each go around in their own circle – starting by going downstage and then out to their own side – and end up back at centre stage. When they touch hands they transform back into* **May** *and* **Joe**.

Scene Three

The first carousel

May and **Joe** *practise the basic step – back step, triple step, triple step.*

May *doesn't know what she is doing so is a little embarrassed and frustrated.* **Joe** *is more practised at the steps and laughs with her whenever they get it wrong. After about four tries they both look up as if they are hearing the* **Teachers** *say something to get their attention, then both say:*

Both   Annnd change partner.

They move apart/change position on a step and then become the first of many couples in the dance class, all trying, and most failing, to dance the basic step together. Most of these couples take a rock step back on the 'Change partners' and triple step into the new pairing.

The first couple they become is **Sally** *and* **George**.

Sally   See it took him an extra week, George, so he wanted to charge me more, de pig, so I said go way outta that, I said, we agreed a price, I said, it's not my fault you're slow. He was ragin' with that, so I threw him a few cans of beer so he was delighted with that.

But ya wanna see the place, George, it's immacula', second to none!

George   Here, Sally, I woulda done that for ya for the few cans.

And an aul root around your house. See where the bodies are buried.

She laughs uproariously.

George   Seriously though, you should have called me.

Sally   Ah ya know me, George, I like to fly solo.

George   Jaysus – Maverick.

She laughs uproariously.

George   I could be your Iceman. Two of us flying around in the skies 'n' all.

And I could come along in me white suit, while you're doing your sewing 'n' all, sweepin' you off your feet 'n' all, carry ya out of the factory with all the girls clapping?

Sally (*starts to laugh uproariously but stops*)   You're mixing up two different fillums there, George.

George   Speaking of fillums, I was thinking . . . would you like to go to the movies on Saturday night?

Sally   Emmmm.

George   Ahh now, Kiki Dee – Don't go breaking me heart.

Sally   Change partners.

As she says 'Change partners', they rock step back and triple step to a new position. In doing so they become the next characters in the carousel, **Rough Guy** *and* **Terrified Girl**. *This is repeated at the end of each dancing couple.*

Rough Guy *sings 'Let's Twist Again' in a very rough manner as he looks to grab passing women to have a dance. It is obvious from his movements that no one is having a bar of him.*

Terrified Girl *realises that he is probably the next person she is supposed to dance with – not an inviting prospect.*

*Still singing, he spots her and grabs her. She may say '*Jesus!'

He twists her roughly by the hand, singing the second half of the chorus.

He then swings her around in a very wide arc singing the middle eight, almost breaking her arm off at the shoulder in the process until he deposits her upstage right.

*He then goes downstage left and proceeds to take a run and jump at her. She screams '*CHANGE PARTNERS!' *and as he lands they turn into* **Regina** *and* **Sean**.

Sean (*slightly under his breath*)   5, 6, 7, 8, 9, 10, 11, 12.

Regina   Is this your first time?

Sean   Eh, yeah.

Regina   Aye, I can tell.

Sean   Lovely, lovely, lovely . . . Jaysus, you're very good.

She nods.

Sean   Right . . . What's your name?

Regina (*sighs*)   Regina.

Sean   Right . . . Em, my name's Sean.

Regina   Nice to meet you, Sean.

Sean   Lovely, lovely, lovely.

They dance on. He may copy her style of dancing (*her outstretched hand for example*).

Em, listen. Maybe you could give me a dance in the social afterwards, teach me one or two of those moves?

Regina   Sorry, no, I don't dance with beginners.

Sean   Oh . . . Lovely, lovely, lovely (*Not lovely at all.*) . . . Change partners.

They become **Justin** *and* **Imelda**.

Justin *is telling* **Imelda**, *who he has never met before, about his Sunday night and dancing a sort of salsa while she just sways back and forth watching him in wonder and awe. He may be the first gay person she has met since she moved to Dublin from Cork.*

Justin   Well, we started in Pantibar where she was *a-ma-zing*!

Then a bunch of us headed up to the George for cocktails and bingo. Full house!

We ended up in the Dragon. Do *not* ask me what happened up there!

As Ronan says – you say it best, when you say . . . (*He does a mime of locking his lips and throwing away the key.*)

Imelda (*realising*)   Are you gay?

Justin (*disgusted*)   Change partners.

Imelda *continues dancing on her own at first. Then a* **Geeky Guy** *spots her, slicks down his hair and walks over to her to ask her to dance. When she spots him coming towards her with his hands out to dance she backs away and shrieks.*

Imelda   It's only my first time!

She dances on her own for a moment. He dances on his own for a moment. They are both just sort of swaying.

He goes towards her again.

I'm not really into dancing!

I only came cos my friend told me it was a good place to meet fellas.

(*Angry, in direction of friend.*) She's full of it!

I mean look at the place.

It's full of aul lads . . .

He looks around and kinda nods. She then looks at him.

And nerds . . .

He realises that she is talking about him. They look at each other.

Change partners.

They become **Noelia** *and* **Uncomprehending Guy**.

Noelia'*s speech is very fast and hard to understand, with a strong Spanish accent. But she also says certain things like 'Oh my God' and 'Dublin' and 'Shite' in a strong Dublin accent. He hasn't a clue what she is saying but is listening out for moments in the conversation that he may have to give a response to, and then pretending to understand them.*

Noelia   I was like, oh my God what language is everybody speaking? My friend said, Noelia, It's the Gaeltacht. They are speaking Irish. I was like oh my God, cos I have been living here twelve years and you never hear it, right?

Uncomprehending Guy (*he has no idea what she has just said but knows it was a question*)   Yeah.

Noelia   Get me back to Dublin where at least I can understand what people are saying! You know?

Uncomprehending Guy   Yeah.

Noelia   Plus, like, Kerry is so nice but Dublin is better. It's better to be in the city, no?

Uncomprehending Guy   Yeah.

Noelia   Yeah. Hey, my name is Noelia, what is your name?

Uncomprehending Guy   . . . Tuesday.

Noelia   Change partners.

They become **Stinky Arm Guy** *and* **Choking Girl**.

Stinky Guy *thinks he is very, very cool. He is dancing away on his own and giving the eye to fellow dancers* (*in the audience*).

He spots **Choking Girl**. *He slicks back his hair.*

Choking Girl   Cool.

He then does a mime of a fishing line being cast out and reels the girl in. She plays along slightly embarrassed.

Girl (*playing along*)   Oooo.

He pulls her in close but when he lifts his arm up she smells the BO. It is terrible.

Oh Jesus.

Another move and she smells it again.

That's terrible.

Again.

I can taste it!

Again.

Smells like bins.

Again.

(*She holds her breath as long as she can and then, choking:*)
Change partner.

They go straight into **Robert** *and* **Terrified Girl**.

Robert *is holding* **Terrified Girl***'s hands and looking up at the
teachers for instructions. She looks terrified. He turns around and
barks into her face.*

Robert   Relax! Relax! Just relax! You can't do it unless you
relax!

Bit of dancing and he looks at teachers.

Robert   Relax . . . Tension . . . You've got to be relaxed . . .
Tension.

*She relaxes her shoulders and tenses them as per instruction. It
doesn't make for enjoyable dancing.*

Bit more dancing as he looks at teachers.

Robert   Look at me, I'm relaxed. I can't relax unless you
relax. WILL YA JUST BUCKIN' RELAX!

Terrified Girl   Change partners!

Scene Four

The first 'back to the Teachers'

Teacher 1 (*male*)   Well done everybody!

Teacher 2 (*female*)   Amazeballs! Now do stick around, the
social is starting now.

Teacher 1   We'll be playing music until 11. So don't be shy, get up and practise those funking moves.

As he finishes this line, the teachers turn upstage. **Teacher 2** *turns back downstage as* **May** *– standing at her chair looking around and wondering if someone is going to ask her to dance, or if she should ask someone.* **Joe** *stays facing upstage with his head in his bag, looking for his towel.*

Music – 'Boogie for Two Fingers'.

Scene Five

The first social

The music starts and there is relative peace.

May *has a think about it and decides she is leaving.*

Joe *doesn't notice this at first as he is towelling himself down.*

She puts on her jacket and gets her bag. She is almost out the door when he spots her.

Joe   Whoa, whoa, whoa, where are ya going?

May (*she is surprised that he is stopping her as she doesn't know him*)   Me?

Joe   Yeah.

May   Ah I'm not getting this at all. I'm going to head off.

Joe   Ya can't go now. Ya gotta stay for the social! That's where you really learn how to dance. By dancing with everyone.

May   No I'm driving everyone mad because I can't get it.

Joe   I'll tell you what. Stay and have one dance with me and then you can leave, guilt free. Just gimme a second to catch me breath. Deal?

May (*after a think*)   Deal.

She comes back into the room.

May   On your own head be it.

He laughs at this and then there is a bit of awkward silence as he continues to towel off and she just waits for the promised dance.

May   Have you been coming here long?

Joe   No, I just started last term.

May   Oh. I saw you dancing earlier. You're very good.

Joe   As Confucius once said, 'He who starts at the beginning is often the last to leave'.

May   Oh. Cool. (*Thinks.*) Did Confucius say that?

Joe   No.

C'mere, you strike me more of the Ceili type. What brings you to swing?

May   I don't know really. My boyfriend is away for three months.

Joe   Prison?

May   No! (*Laughs.*) He's working abroad. So I was at a bit of a loose end. Always thought I'd try it at some stage.

Joe   *Trés bien!*

May   What about you? What made you come?

Joe   Oh, emm, do ya want the long story or the short story?

May   The short story, I'm only staying for one dance!

Joe   Yeah, good choice – If you look out that window, there's a building across the street. For 23 years I sat looking out at yoga, lunchtime theatre, swing. Eventually I took the plunge, came over, took the place by storm.

May   So I see.

Joe *gets up to dance.*

Joe   Come on, let's give it a *swing* . . . See what I did there . . .

May   Oh, I did.

Joe   Aaand 5, 6, 7, 8.

They go to dance but she tries to lead straight away.

Joe (*siren noise 1 – ambulance – wooo whoo*)

May   . . .?

Joe (*siren noise 2 – klaxon horn – ehaaw ehaaw*)

May   What?

Joe   You're leading.

May   Everyone's giving out to me for that!

Joe   Well, the idea is, the man leads, and the woman follows.

She drops his hands.

May   Why?

Joe   Because otherwise it just doesn't work. Aristotle said 'Humans are by nature a social animal'. Therefore there have to be rules otherwise there would be chaos.

May   Aristotle never said that!

Joe (*Laughing.*)   Emmmm. He did actually.

May   Ok, but, societies change, rules change. So I don't see why the man should always lead.

Joe   Ok, good point. Well, think about it like an offer. I offer that we do it this way and if you choose to accept, we dance well together.

May   Ok I accept. Just don't *lead* me astray . . . See what I did there?

Joe   Oh, I did.

And, 5, 6, 7, 8.

They start dancing again but this time she has no tension in her arm and their connection is limp. She has no 'frame'.

Joe   Ok, think of yourself as a big overloaded shopping trolley.

May   What!!

Joe   I'm shopping, I'm shopping, I'm shopping. I realise I've forgotten something. I pull the shopping trolley back. But it's got its own momentum, it resists. Keep that bit of resistance. And it comes with me. I grab the tin of peas . . .

And then I go forward again but now I need to work against the trolleys momentum. I push you forward, keep going, keep going, until I pull you back again.

May   O . . . k . . .

Joe   So keep that tension and let's try the rock step again. 5, 6, 7, 8.

They dance.

May (*eventually . . . with a laugh*)   I'm getting it!

Joe   Of course you are.

They do this for ten seconds or so. It's enjoyable.

Joe   Look over my left shoulder there.

May   What am I looking at?

Joe   Gerald and Julia. They've been dancing together for forty years.

They never talk. They don't need to.

May   They're doing a slower version.

They slow down and start to come together . . .

Joe   Beautiful . . .

When they come together, they dance as **Gerald** *and* **Julia** *for about twenty seconds. As they transform into* **Gerald** *and* **Julia***, the step transforms into a slow blues step.*

This ends when they separate and both look down to their hands, which are held together. They are **Joe** *and* **May** *again. They stop holding hands.*

May   Thanks.

What's your name?

Joe   Joe.

She extends her hand.

May   I'm May.

He takes it.

Lights down. **May** *and* **Joe** *swap seats, taking their bags and coats with them during the scene break.*

Act Two

Scene One

Pe-class

Lights back up. **Joe** *and* **May** *are getting ready for class again (jackets, water, towels, etc.). They spot each other.*

Joe   Ya came back! Good on ya!

May   I've been dreaming about shopping trolleys.

Joe   That'll pass. Do ya remember the step?

May   The basic step? Yeah, (*She demonstrates.*) rock step /

Both   / triple and your triple and a rock step, triple and your /

They snap into the **Teachers** *on a step-out. Again, the* **Teachers'** *hands may shoot up in the air to get everyone's attention.*

Scene Two

The second Teachers' scene

Teacher 2   Welcome back to week two everybody!

Teacher 1   Nice to see so many of you came back! Now this week, we're going to start off with a little warm-up.

Teacher 2   He loves this bit!

Teacher 1 (*snaps*)   What's not to love.

Ok, everyone give me jazz hands. Come on! Let me see those jazz hands! Up high, in the sky, down low, too slow!

As he goes from high to low, he speeds up and catches **Teacher 2** *out.*

Teacher 2   It's not a competition.

Teacher 1 (*hurrying her along*)   Do the monkey walk.

Teacher 2   Now everyone do the monkey walk! Monkey walk everybody! I love *this* one!

Teacher 1   Suits you.

Teacher 2   Piss off!

Teacher 1   Oh! (*Sings the opening line of 'I Wan'na Be like You' from* The Jungle Book.)

Teacher 2 *is about to go on to the next part of the warm-up but* **Teacher 1** *keeps going with his song, singing the second line.*

Teacher 2 (*hurrying him along*)   Fish bums!

Teacher 1   Now give me your fish bums. (*Shakes bum and moves backwards.*) Fish bums, people! Shake your tail feather, you! Put her into reverse you! Beep beep beep . . .

They collide.

Teacher 2   I think they're ready! Ready for . . .

Both   THE LINDY HOP!

Teacher 2   Now it's like the basic step we did last week, except this time instead of a six count (*Dramatic pause.*) . . . it's an eight count . . .

Both (*fake scream of fear*)   AAAAAH!

Teacher 2   So you've got your rock step, triple . . . step step, triple that's rock step, triple, step step triple!

Teacher 1   You're supposed to count it!

Teacher 2   Yes I was about to! And you can count it out. 1, 2, 3 and 4, 5, 6, 7 and 8. Amazebeams! Ok find a partner and let's do this.

Teacher 1   And 5, 6, 7, 8.

They go around in a circle. When they meet up again in the middle they have changed into **Joe** *and* **Sally**.

Scene Three

The second carousel

In this carousel **Joe** *dances with various females in the class.*

Straight into the lindy hop.

Sally   Ah, Joe!

Joe   Howya, Sally!

Bit of dancing.

May   Did ya go to Bloom?

Joe   I did yeah.

May   25 euro in?! I NEARLY GOT SICK! And I went the three days so it cost me 75. Jesus tonight. I won't be going again.

Bit of dancing.

Sally   C'mere, I went up to the Botanic Gardens the other day looking for you!

Joe   Ah did ya, Sally?

Sally   I did, yeah, I was talking to this horrible-looking yoke with red hair, do ya know him?

Joe   I do yeah . . .

Sally   I said to him EXCUSE ME, I said, where would I find the horticulture students.

Oh says he – who are ya looking for?

Says I – me friend Joe.

Says he – why?

Says I – I want to get some of the veg from your organic garden there.

Oh says he – ya can't get any of that!

Says I – WHY?!

Well, he'd no answer to that, de pig!

Sure, yiz probably throw them out, do yiz, Joe?

Joe   I'll tell you what, come up to me on Saturday evening, Sally, I'll throw ya a few.

Sally   Ah that's no use! I'm going to see a Rod Stewart tribute band with George on Saturday.

Joe   Whoo! (*Looking over at* **George**.) You and George at long last.

Sally   What?! Don't be stupid, Joe. I'm not interested in anything like that. I fly solo. We're just friends.

Joe *sings the chorus from the Rod Stewart song 'You're In My Heart'*

Sally   Now stop that, Joe, you'll be giving him ideas!

Joe *keeps singing.*

Sally   I'm serious.

When **Joe** *reaches the word 'lover', he points at George extravagantly.'*

Sally   You're after annoying me now. Aaa! Change partners.

She becomes **Noelia**.

Noelia   So nice to dance with you, Joe, you are really good, easy to follow.

Little dance, possibly a little flourish as she kicks her foot out.

Joe   How's the new job, Noelia? Google isn't it?

Noelia   *Si.* It's ok. A little bit lonely maybe. In my old job, there were a lot of other people who spoke my language – now, not so much. (*Dub accent on 'much'.*) And most of my friends have gone home.

Joe   Ah, you're not thinking of going home are you?

Noelia   No, Joe, no way. I love to live in Dublin. You Irish people are always giving out, oh it's a kip and all this shite, but it's a great place to be, even now. The people are good people for the most part. Like, go to my home town and try to get a job, you will know all about it.

Joe   Yeah. No, it is a good aul spot.

Noelia   It's a good aul spot, Joe!

They have a little laugh at this.

And change partners.

She becomes **Regina**.

She dances in a very controlled way. It doesn't look very joyful, especially for **Joe**.

Regina   Nice job, Joe, well done.

Joe   I think we are getting the hang of it, Regina.

Regina   Well I've actually done it before. Frankly, I'm getting a bit tired of them going over the same old ground.

Joe   I find it helpful.

Regina   Well you haven't been coming as long as I have. Sometimes I have to dance with absolute IDIOTS! (*Shouts this at someone dancing close to them.*) Very frustrating! People shouldn't be allowed to just walk in willy-nilly.

Joe   Yeah, they should be vetted at the door.

Regina   Absolutely.

Joe   Oh, Jesus (*looking away quickly under his breath*).

Regina   That's what I said.

Nice job, Joe. Well done. Change partners.

She becomes **Imelda**.

Joe *goes to dance with her and she backs off shrieking.*

Imelda   It's only my second time!

They never tell you what to do with your hands. I've seen you, you're very good. I like the way you do your hands.

He goes to dance with her again but she backs off again.

Imelda   I'm supposed to be going to Australia really soon anyway, so . . .

Imelda *starts to (sort of) dance a large circle around him during this next section.*

Joe   Oh, one of my sons is in Australia.

She stops dancing.

Imelda   No, way, give me his number.

Joe   Eh, ok.

She continues dancing her circle.

Imelda   Are you married?

Joe   Eh, not anymore.

Imelda   Did she die?

Joe   Eh no, we broke up.

Imelda   What do you do?

Joe   I'm back in college.

She stops dancing again.

Imelda (*he may now be an object of slight pity/disgust*)   You're a student!

Joe   Yep.

She starts again.

Imelda   Why? Did you lose your job?

Joe   Yeah, I did.

Imelda   Because of the recession.

Joe   Yeah, I suppose.

Imelda   So did my dad, he'd a nervous breakdown . . . Did you have a nervous breakdown?

Joe   Eh, no . . . Not yet.

How's your dad now? Is he back on track?

Imelda   No, he never leaves the shed. It drives my mother mad. Just sits there staring out at her.

Give me your son's number!

Joe   Eh . . .

Imelda (*with urgency*)   Come here, who's that young fella my friend's talking to! Change partners.

She takes three steps and on the third step she lifts her arms and becomes **Teacher 2**.

Scene Four

The second 'back to the Teachers'

Teacher 2   Great work everybody! Amazebums! Now, as always, we play music until 11.

Teacher 1   This is where you step it up and step it out so do stick around and boogie on down you crazy cats!

Music comes on.

Scene Five

The second social

May *watches* **Joe** *as he indicates to someone* (*in the audience*) *that he will dance with them as soon as he cools down a bit.* (*He may do a bit of a trumpet mime to a trumpet blast in the music.*)

May   You're a popular guy.

Joe   Oh yeah, I'm a babe magnet. And when that magnet is turned on . . .

He does a mime (with some sound . . .) of him being a magnet and women flying past him and then sticking to his forehead, chest and legs.

May   Seems to be off now. I'd say you're safe enough.

Joe *laughs as all the mimed women fall off his person on to the ground with a 'whump'.*

May   So can you fit me in?

Joe   I think I can squeeze you in. Lemme just . . . (*Indicates the towel.*) whoo! (*He towels.*) How are you getting on?

May   I'm really glad I came back. I wasn't sure if I would.

Joe   But here you are.

May   Here I am.

Beat.

May *looks up at the window they referred to in Scene One.*

May   . . . Do you ever see any of your colleagues staring down at you.

Joe   Hmmmm? Oh, I'm not there anymore. *They're* not there anymore.

May   Oh.

Joe   No, belly up. Kapoot. Finito binito.

May   What kind of business was it?

Joe   It was a printing company. My father set it up. Ah, we upgraded at the wrong time maybe – just as things went digital. Should have seen it coming. People could send their order to The Netherlands and have it delivered, quicker than us, cheaper than us, better quality than us.

May   That's tough.

Joe Yeah. It was tough for a while. A few very dark years.

Realising he is being a bit heavy with someone he hardly knows.

But I have emerged blinking into the light again. And here I am, King of Swing . . . oh, and every blooming thing.

May Every blooming thing?

Joe I've gone back to college. Horticulture. Botanic Gardens.

May Very nice! You're a noddy.

Joe . . .?

May A noddy! (*Nods her head vigorously like a diligent student*) A mature student.

Joe (*laughing at this joke*) Not that mature. I've only just decided what I want to be when I grow up. Actually that's not true – many, *many* years ago, I knew exactly what I wanted to be.

May Yeah?

Joe I went to America. I made it to thirty-eight of the fifty states. Most of it on a motorcycle.

Bought it for 470 bucks. Stripped it down. Sprayed it khaki green. Strapped all me gear to it. Went across the Southern States – Louisiana, Mississippi, New Mexico.

May Wow!

Joe Ran out of money in Eureka, Northern California.

May Eureka! Jesus, when I went to America on a J-1 we just spent the summer getting drunk on Virginia Beach.

Joe Ragin' I missed that now!

May Go on anyway, what did you do in Eureka?

Joe   I was a forest ranger. Loved it! Drove a dodge pick-up, with a bench seat, all around the Redwood forest. Magnificent – a cathedral of trees.

Learnt about seedlings, reforestation, timber. I remember thinking – this is it – I'm a lumberjack and I'm ok.

May   So then, why did ya come back?

Joe   Ah . . . (*Again he makes the decision to go on.*) the call from home, my father wasn't well.

Someone had to look after the business. So I stood in, thinking all the time, 'I'll get back to the trees when I sort this out'.

Then I met Marie. We fell in love . . . Sliding doors . . .

Next thing, we're married, two kids, it's twenty-three years later. The Company's going down the drain and I'm staring out the window wondering should I jump . . . Or go dancing!

May   And ya came dancing?

Joe   Yeah but it took me a while to get across that street. There were a few roundabouts and potholes along the way. But then, once the boys moved to America and Australia /
. . .

May   / My brother's in Sydney!

Joe   The Opera House, lovely! Luke was there for a while. He's in Perth now. The other fellow, Matthew, is in Chicago.

May   And will they come home?

Joe   Ah, they think they will. But ya know how these things happen. They'll meet a girl and the next thing we're all heading over for the wedding.

May   My brother'll never come home. We really miss him. But there just isn't anything here for him. He had a shitty job, with an hour-long commute. Over there, he walks to work in the sunshine by the Harbour Bridge! Sure how can we compete?

Small beat.

Joe   The Port Tunnel?

May (*laughing*)   He's more ambitious over there.

Joe   Some places just seem to suit people. Or people suit places.

May   At least there's Skype. Though it's always a bit of an event, the call, isn't it? Ya have to have your stories ready. Sometimes when I haven't seen him for a while, and his face comes up, I burst out crying . . .

Joe   Oh no.

May   No, not good! Do you talk to your boys often?

Joe   Ah ya know lads. I leave them messages on the landline. They do the same. We play a lot of phone tag.

May   And do you and your wife ever go over?

Joe   Ah, we're not together anymore.

May   Oh, sorry.

Joe   No, she's good. *We're* good. We're getting on with it . . . I think.

Anyway, come here – what about you?

He crosses to the stage-left chair to tie his laces.

Ya doing your leaving cert?

May *laughs.*

Joe   Your mocks?

May (*laughing*)   I'm a graphic designer.

Joe   Very good!

May   It's pretty good. It's quieter than it used to be.

Joe   So you're a graphic designer and you're ok. (*Like the lumberjack above.*)

May   Yeah . . . (*Considers.*) Well I was going to be an artist . . . but . . . ah it didn't work out.

Joe   Oh?

May   I still do a bit at home.

Joe   And yer fella, the one in prison, is he an artist too?

May   Oh God no. He's a project manager.

Joe   What does he manage?

May   Emmm . . . Projects?

Joe   . . . Bing! Come on we'll dance. The lindy hop!

They come together and she roughly grips his hands.

Ok. Barbie hands.

May   What?

Joe   Barbie hands.

He puts his hands so that they are horizontal to the ground, relaxed but slightly curved downwards – the Barbie hands.

May *copies this . . . but also makes a Barbie face.*

Joe   Barbie hands, not Barbie face.

She laughs and relaxes her face. They start to dance. And they dance well together.

May   Check me out!

Joe   Check you out!

Swell in the music. He throws in a few fancy moves, swinging her, etc. She is loving it.

They ad-lib stuff like **May** *– 'I'm gonna fall off' and* **Joe** *– 'You stayed on!'*

The music comes back down.

May   And come here, ya did all that travelling on your own?

Joe   I did yeah. Ah most people were going to Boston and New York. I just wanted to go into the wild . . . Texas. The Wild West!

May   Texas! We all just followed a template. J-1, Virginia Beach, working in bars.

Joe   That's fun too.

May   Yeah but, like, no one went off on their own, looking for a real adventure.

Joe   Well, do it now?

May   Aaaahhh, it's too late now. I'm nearly forty! I've a job . . . a partner.

Joe   Well what about the art? The bit at home. What kind of stuff do ya do?

May   Oh, emmm, portraits mostly. Stuff for friends. Wedding presents.

Joe   Lovely! Caricatures. (*He does a little mime of a guy doing a caricature . . . He is messing with her.*)

May   No! They're like photo-realistic portraits. Well that's what I try to do.

Joe   Wow! Sounds difficult!

May   Yeah, yeah it is actually.

Joe   And do you sell them?

May   No, no! They're just for friends.

Joe   Exhibitions?

May   Oh God no!

Joe   And . . . would you sell them if someone wanted to buy them?

May   Ah they wouldn't want to. I haven't really kept it up enough to develop my own style.

Joe   Yeah . . . but that's not really what I asked. (*This is gentle and encouraging.*)

May   I'm a good amateur is all.

Joe   Again, not really what I asked.

May   It's not that easy!

Joe   Ok, well that's that then.

May   Ah Joe, stop bullying me! It's alright for you! You're back at college doing something you love!

Joe   I'm fifty. How did that happen?! I've lost the house. I've lost the wife. I'm in a bedsit. (*Realising what he sounds like.*) . . . Jesus I'm a country and western song . . .

I'm struggling!

But I'm here. I'm dancing. I'm smiling.

May   You are.

Joe   I am.

After a couple of seconds – lights down.

Act Three

Scene One

The third pre-class

When lights come back up **Joe** *is rushing into the class. He is late.*
May *spots him . . .*

They may whisper during this next section.

May (*calling him over to her*) Joe, Joe.

Joe Close one! (*Referring to the fact that he is almost late.*)
Howya doing?

May Good. How was the exam?

Joe Great, nearly didn't make it here. I haven't even
showered!

May Get away from me!

Joe So what's new, pussycat – (*Sings the next part.*) whoa
whoa a whoa?

May Not much, pussycat. I didn't go into work today.

Joe Oh . . . So you're floating around in your slippers
all day?

May Yeah, well, Simon came home.

Joe Oh, the boyfriend?

May Yeah.

Joe Very nice.

May Yeah. But I did a good bit of painting.

Joe Very good. That's what I like to hear.

Ok, Frida Kahlo, enough of the chit chat, I need to focus. I
think we're doing the Charleston tonight.

May   Oh, brudder!

She starts singing the Charleston song 'Ba ba, ba ba, ba' . . . he joins in . . . they don't know what they are doing – they are doing their own version of what they think the Charleston is. On a cue in the Charleston they are singing they become the **Teachers**.

Scene Two

The third Teachers' scene

Teacher 2   Ok, guys, we're six weeks in and everybody is really coming along!

Teacher 1 *goes in front of* **Teacher 2** *and points at* **May**. *In doing so he nearly takes* **Teacher 2**'s *head off. During this section they move around and pick out different people in the audience/places in the room and direct the praise/guidance at these areas.*

Teacher 1   May, you've improved so much! But you've got to stop trying to lead.

Teacher 2   Sean, you're fantastic but maybe its time to stop counting out loud.

Teacher 1   Imelda /

Teacher 2 (*snaps*)   Regina!

Teacher 1 (*snaps*)   They look the same! Regina, great! But you've got to loosen up.

Teacher 2   Justin, get rid of those salsa hips. Otherwise, amazalicious!

Teacher 1   Imelda – do try to keep some sort of contact with your partners during the dances.

Teacher 2 (*as if* **Noelia** *is deaf or stupid*) No-e-lia . . . Ab-sol-ute-ly gor-geous!

Teacher 1   Lovely, George and Sally. Great partnership.

Teacher 2   But everyone! Seriously! Great work!

Teacher 1   Ok, tonight we're going to have a go at the Charleston! So let's get down to busyness.

Teacher 2   Business

Teacher 1   Busyness.

Leads back on your left.

Follows back on your right.

She interrupts him as he is about to do the next section, much to his annoyance.

Teacher 2   And it's back, forward, kick and down.

That's . . . Back, forward, kick and down. Opposite leg, watch me. WATCH ME!

Kick, two, three and down on the fourth.

Teacher 1   That's . . . Kick, two, three and down on the fourth.

Let's put that together. And 5, 6, 7, 8.

Both   Back, forward, kick and down.

Kick, kick, kick and down.

Back, forward, kick and down

Kick, kick, kick, and down.

Teacher 2   Absolutely amazoids!! Ok, now look up here for some variations.

They do this next section of variations quite quickly. It is hard to imagine people picking up the steps in this time.

So you've got your back, forward, kick and down and you can do a slap down on your left on the second beat, you can do a criss cross, /

Teacher 1   / you can do a turn on the five, in fact, you can both turn on the five and meet back together for the rock step on the one!

Teacher 2   Everyone got that?

No one has got this. But the teachers are blissfully unaware of this.

Teacher 1   Ok! Find a partner. Let's do this.

Scene Three

The third carousel

In this carousel **May** *dances with various males in the class.*

George *is looking straight out and seems completely bewildered by the previous instruction.*

George   Ah here!

He looks around; people seem to be starting to try the step. Looks back at **May**.

George   Alright, May – bit of the aul Charleston. Jaysus – do I have to do this and talk at the same time!

May   You don't have to talk, Georgie!

George   Right yeah! C'mere, hold on a second . . .

Goes over to someone else in the class (front row of the audience).

Come here, back off there, buddy, we're all sharing the floor!

He goes back to **May**, *but stares the offender out of it. He might even do a thing with his elbows and say 'What's all that about?!'*

They start to Charleston.

George   And we're off!

They Charleston together for a few steps. He can be quite comical in his older man confident way of dancing.

He spots **Sally**.

George   Look at her over there. Sally! She's only gorgeous!

Took her out the other night to see me Hoops playing the Bohs. (*He re-creates the football match by breaking free from* **May**, *stopping the imaginary ball with his chest and scoring the goal*.) Ball in, chest, on the volley, back of the net! One nil! Schilllllaciiiooooow! (*He rejoins her for the dance*.) then on to the Parnell Mooney. Roof garden. Brandy and lime. A few packets of crips. Lovely aul night.

May   Did ya get a kiss?

George (*forceful*)   Course I got a kiss! (*Backing down*.) Well a peck on the cheek. She can't resist me.

May   Sure who could, George?

George   Thinking of asking her to go away with me for the weekend. (*Slightly aggressive and possibly looking her up and down*.) You! As a woman – What do you think?

May   Emmmm . . .

George   I've already booked it.

May   Without asking her?!

George   Well, women like that. Decisiveness 'n' all. Sweepin' 'em off their feet!

May   I dunno George . . . Go easy. Women prefer to be part of the decision I think.

George   Ya what?! (*Disgusted*.) Change partners.

He becomes **Sean**.

Sean (*counting slightly out loud*)   5, 6, 7, 8, 9, 10, 11, 12, 13, 14, 15, 16, 17.

May   Sean, will we count it out together? So we can stay on the same beat, be easier.

Sean   Oh, ok. Lovely, lovely, lovely. You start, you start.

May   5, 6, 7, 8, 1, 2, 3, 4 . . .

Sean   *He counts with her . . . but he keeps going . . .* 9, 10, 11, 12 . . . up to 16.

As he starts to get it.

Sean (*excited*)   Oh lovely, lovely, lovely! I'm getting it! I'm getting it!

May   Good man, Sean!

Sean   Ah fuck it! I've lost it! I've lost it!

May   You're well able for it. We'll start again.

5, 6, 7, 8, 1, 2, 3, 4 . . .

They start again. He keeps counting (under his breath).

Sean, how come you never stay for the social?

Sean   Ahh no, that's more for the advanced dancers.

May   Not at all! That's where you learn – by dancing with other people.

Stay for it tonight.

Sean   Ah no.

May   Do.

Sean   No I don't think so.

May   Ah do. Give me a dance?

He looks at her. Delighted.

Sean   I will so. I will May . . . Lovely, lovely, lovely.

May   Lovely.

Sean (*looking towards the* **Teachers** *who are telling them to move on to the next person*)   Ah really?

(*Disappointed.*) We've to change partners.

She dances away in a circle.

Sean *becomes* **Robert**.

Robert (*holding* **May***'s hands and looking at the* **Teachers** *rather than her*)   RELAX, MAY, RELAX!

May   Robert!

Robert   WHY DON'T YOU JUST RELAX!

May   Robert, stop telling me to relax. I can't possibly relax if you keep telling me.

Robert   MAYBE YOU COULD JUST RELAX? TENSION!

May   You're making me tense.

Robert   RELAX!

May   Let the girl be tense. Let it happen.

Robert   JUST RELAX!

May   ROBERT! You relax! (*Calm.*)

She turns him around. His shoulders visibly relax. He relaxes. Big relaxed face. They dance for a moment in this new state of relaxation.

Robert (*very relaxed*)   Change partners.

He becomes **Justin**.

Justin   So, May, I hear somebody's fella's back in town.

May   Who told ya that?

Justin   A little birdy told me . . . (*Then mouths 'Joe, Joe told me' as he points over at* **Joe**.)

May   Oh . . .

Justin   Did ya jump his bones the minute he opened the door?

May   Emm no, Justin, I didn't.

Justin   Exsqueeze me?

May   We're past all that – we've been together for three years.

Justin   He's been away for three months!

May   I know but he was starving.

Justin   Roar! – (*Tiger noise and ripping away Simon's clothes.*)

May   We just had breakfast!

They dance on for a beat.

Justin   Did he at least bring you back a gorgeous present? (*he indicates the engagement ring finger without her noticing*)

May   Yes! He brought me back a CD of Peruvian music.

He stops.

Justin   Pan pipes? . . .

She stops.

May   Yeah

Justin   . . . Change partners.

He takes two steps away from her and then they both lift their arms in the air to become the **Teachers**.

Scene Four

The third 'back to the Teachers'

Teacher 2   Do stick around for the social, folks. We've got a new DJ playing tonight . . .

DJ Johnnie B Bad will be rocking the house!

Teacher 1   Yeah! Keeping it for realz!

He does a mortifying and inappropriate gesture appropriated from African American ghetto culture. **Teacher 2** *gives him a shocked look and as they turn away they become* **Joe** *and* **May**.

Scene Five

The third social

Music comes on – Charleston.

May *is practicing the Charleston and she is actually quite good.*

Joe   I see you doing the Charleston, May. You're a natural!

May   The pupil has become the master.

Joe   So the master has fallen, eh? Well we won't get carried away.

May   So the exam was ok?

Joe   Good, yeah. I think?

May   When do you get the results?

Joe   Oh, emmm, a few weeks I suppose. After Easter.

May   Great.

Beat. She practises away.

Joe   You must be delighted to have, emmmm, Simon home?

She runs out of steam and takes a seat during the next line or two.

May   Yeah. Weird having him back. Ya kinda get used to your own space.

Beat.

Joe   You guys together long?

May   A few years. But we knew each other for a long time before that. His brother is a good friend of mine.

Joe   And he's a . . . good guy?

May   Ah yeah. He's a really good guy.

She sort of stops at this point. The wind is out of her sails. This is not a big gesture.

Beat.

Joe   Are you ok?

May   Ah no, I'm fine.

Joe   Ya sure?

May   Yeah . . . Ah it was just a bit of an anti-climax. Him coming home today.

Joe   Right.

Beat.

He's not interested in coming along to the classes?

May   God no! He'd be too self-conscious.

Beat.

We don't really do anything together. Sometimes I think we're just staying in it out of laziness.

Joe   And are yis? Staying in it out of laziness?

May   Ah no, no, I just said that. Don't mind me.

She gets up.

Come on, let's dance.

The music swells as they dance the Charleston for a bit. They do a swivel. They separate.

Poor aul Simon. I'll tell you this, he's a lot better than most of the dzopes out there.

Joe   Dzopes! . . . (*A la Joe* **Duffy***, maybe with a hand over the ear as if there is a headphone held up against it.*) We're talking about dzopes you've been with. Go ahead, caller, you're live on air. Dzopes – over to you!

She gets the joke and goes with it.

May   Ok, Joe.

Joe   Talk to Joe!

May   Well there was the French guy I met in Paris.

Joe   Jaysus, Jaysus, a French guy? In Paris? Unbelievable!

May   And we were having a lovely time . . . until I found out he was married!

Joe   . . . uh oh.

May   And it wasn't the first time he did it.

Joe   A serial adulter-er-er . . .?

May   Yeah! The next fellow stood me up on my birthday, invited me out to make up for it and then . . .

Joe   Stood you up again!

May   Exactly! A serial stander up-er-er . . .! Another chap, a very handsome Swede, brought me to a wedding, where I didn't know anyone /

Joe   Serial killer?

May   No! But he left it with his ex-girlfriend . . .

Joe   No!

May   Leaving me – looking de fool!

Joe   If ya don't mind me saying, May – you certainly seem to pick 'em!

May   Exactly. I couldn't trust my own judgement! And then Simon came along. And . . . he's lovely!

Beat.

He's not married, he's never stood me up and he has never, not even once, left a party, that we were at, with his ex-girlfriend!

Joe   They're three of the things I always look for in a fella.

May   The basics!

Beat.

Joe   It's like . . . It's like, you were walking along – doo de doo, doo de doo, BANG, you get a slap on the head. What the hell was that? But ya picked yourself up – doo de doo, doo de doo and BANG – hit again! But ya kept shimmying along – doo de doo, and then BANG – ah not again!

But ya know what, May, ya have to keep going. Ya have to keep doo de doo-ing.

Beat.

To doo de doo or not to doo de doo, that is the question.

They dance on, then she thinks for a second and stops dancing . . .

May   Are ya saying that I've stopped going doo de doo with Simon?

Joe   Well no . . . he sounds like a good guy.

May   Yeah. Yeah, he is!

Beat.

Mind you, he did just bring me back a CD of pan-pipe music . . .

Joe   O . . . k . . .

May   Anyway I don't need to go doo de doo anymore cos I'm with him!

Joe   Fair enough . . . No more doo de doo.

They dance for a few moments while this settles in.

May   What about you? Are you going doo de doo?

Joe   Ah that's different, May. There's not that much happening on the doo de doo front at my age.

May   Well . . . maybe you should be?

Joe   Maybe . . . (*He looks at her, wondering about the possibilities.*) . . . maybe.

They continue to dance whilst thinking about the doo de doos.

After a couple of seconds – lights down.

Act Four

Scene One

The fourth pre-class

*While the lights are down, **May** and **Joe** both move in a clockwise direction and end up with her slightly more downstage (left) than him. She has slipped on an engagement ring during this move. She doesn't necessarily want him to see the ring. At least not straight away.*

Easter has been between the last class and this one so they haven't seen each other in a couple of weeks. He can't wait to see her but she is being a little shifty with him.

When lights come back on he is in ebullient form. He has been watching out for her and when he spots her he says:

Joe   May! May! (*He sings the Charleston theme and doing the dance.*) Bam bam – bam bam – bam bam . . . I've been practising all Easter!

May   So I see.

Joe   I am Charleston ready! Charleston hot!

May   Good on ya.

Joe   I missed the aul dancing over the break.

May   Yeah, me too.

Joe   Did ya have a good one?

May   (*Nods.*) mmmmh, it was busy. We were down in West Cork. It was pretty full on to be honest.

Joe   Yourself and the convict?

May   And the two families. Pretty full on to be honest.

Joe   I can imagine. Any dancing?

May   No. No there wasn't actually. What did you do?

Joe   I was up in the library a bit. But I spent most of it up in the Gardens.

May   Ah, nice.

Joe   It was. But I woulda preferred being here with me aul dance partner.

May   Yeah . . . yeah.

Joe   And come here / (*Snap into* **Teachers**.)

Scene Two

The fourth Teachers

Teacher 2   Welcome back from the Easter break, everybody!

Teacher 1   This year is the centenary of our hero Frankie Manning's /

Teacher 2 (*screams – à la Beatle mania*)   FRANKIE MANNINGS! /

Teacher 1 (*he is now deaf. Sticking his finger in his ear*)   'Sake! . . . Birth. Frankie Mannings' birth. Now in a few weeks we'll be teaching you the shim sham, which you can all YouTube Frankie doing /

Teacher 2 (*stealing his thunder*)   It's a real treat. Now, in the meantime, we're going to get you up to speed with some of the moves you need to know for the shim sham. We're going to practise the Shorty George.

Teacher 1   Now if anyone here has ever been drunk, you're gonna find this one easy.

Teacher 2   Well you certainly find it easy.

Teacher 1   YOU'RE EASY!

They are both shocked. He recovers.

Teacher 1   . . . So if you can all get in a line.

Teacher 2 (*Still wounded at first . . . but she recovers.*)   So the Shorty George, its like the kick ball change we did a few weeks back – you're going to kick out on your right foot and kick ball change down with the left foot in front and then you're gonna bring the right leg in front like so and you're gonna keep it moving. This is the Shorty George everybody.

She gives a demonstration. Then encourages the class to try it out.

Teacher 2   Give it a go. GIVE IT A GO!!!

AMAZINGTONS!! – I see some great Shorty Georgers!

Teacher 1   And we've also got the boogie walk, now this is a nice one, it's on an 8 count,

Both (*Fake scream of fear.*)   Aaaahh!

Teacher 1   We're gonna slide step, slide step, slide step, here we go. Bring your arms into it. Let's see those hips moving. Get groovy with it. You've got to step it out.

During the demonstration they have moved themselves upstage so that they are in a good position for the next **May** *and* **Joe** *section.*

Teacher 2   Everybody got that? Ok, now give it a go.

Scene Three

The fourth social (there is no carousel in scene 4 or 5))

Music.

May *and* **Joe** *start practising the kick out.*

She may say – 'Don't kick me.' He may laugh at this. They kick out a few times. Then he spots the ring. He stops.

Joe   Is that what I think it is?

She stops.

May   What? (*She knows exactly what he is talking about*.)
Oh yeah.

Joe   Wow!

May   Yeah. He asked me to marry him.

Joe   I can see that. (*He is surprised when he hears the nasty tone/ edge in his own voice*.)

May   Joe. (*She is not sure if he is messing or being mean*.)

Joe   And you said yes?

May   Yes, of course I said yes. Well I could hardly say no.

Joe   No. No you could hardly say no.

He dances forward doing the boogie walk. When he comes back he says:

Joe   Well . . . congratulations.

May   Ah thanks.

She dances forward practising the boogie walk.

Joe   Ya happy?

May   Kinda shocked.

More dancing.

Joe   Ya must be delighted.

May   Well I wasn't expecting it.

Joe   Yeah, I know what you mean.

They dance on.

She changes direction as if instructed by the **Teachers**. *She goes from dancing in an upstage/downstage direction, to a stage-left/ stage-right direction. He also changes direction.*

She tries to get them back on track in their conversation/friendship.

May   How have you been?

Joe   Yeah yeah, tickety boo.

Beat.

May   How are your boys?

Joe   I haven't spoken to them in a while.

May   Yeah, Skype can be tricky sometimes.

Joe (*distractedly*)   Yeah, yeah.

He stops.

Joe   May, are ya sure?

May   What?

Joe (*indicating the ring finger*)   Are ya sure?

May   What kind of a thing is that to ask?

Joe   Well, three weeks ago you didn't seem that sure.

May   Well I am.

She starts to dance again.

Joe   Ok.

He is not convinced. He lets this hang. He starts to dance again.

She stops.

May   Well I don't know. Is anyone? Were you sure when you got married?

Joe   Yes. No. Well as sure as I could be.

May   Well, look how that worked out.

Beat. That was nasty.

Joe   Look, I don't fucking remember to be honest. And it didn't work out. So it's a shit example.

May   Well, there you are . . .

Beat.

I'm sorry. Look, I'm trying to doo de doo.

She is looking for his support but he isn't about to give it.

Joe   A bit of pan-pipe music and everything is ok?

May   *She is annoyed now. And upset.*

May   Joe, that's mean.

Joe   You're banging on one minute about a fellah who won't even come to a dance class with ya and the next you're getting married! You're saying one thing and doing another!

May   I didn't say anything!

Joe   No . . . No . . . ya didn't.

They both start to practise the boogie walk in a temper. After a horizontal pass:

Joe   Very romantic, those pan pipes.

May   Fuck off now, Joe!

She stops.

Jesus! Why can't you just be nice and say congratulations.

He stops

Joe   Because . . . I did say congratulations.

Well done, congratulations.

May   Thanks!

They dance on.

Anyway, I'm not going to be able to come for a while. I'm going to be so busy with the wedding.

Joe   Yeah, serviettes and eehhh placemats . . . Do ya think you'd get those pan-pipe players to play?

She stops. So he stops.

May   Actually do you know what, I'm just going to head off, I've got stuff to do . . .

She gathers up her stuff. He starts to dance again.

Joe   Yeah. I'll see ya.

As she is walking out.

May   Good luck with your exam results.

Joe   Yeah, good luck yourself.

She is gone.

He continues to dance on his own for a few seconds and stops and looks in her direction.

Lights down.

Act Five

Scene One

The fifth pre-class

Lights up. It's the start of the class and **Joe** *is standing centre stage on his own.*

He responds to each of the following recorded voices (V/Os).

New Guy (*V/O*)   Swing? Swing? Is this swing?

Joe *nods yeah and indicates where the* **New Guy** *should go – anywhere.*

Regina (*V/O*)   Jesus, Joe, I didn't come here to look at that face. Cheer up.

George (*V/O*)   Come here, Joe, your friend May never came back!

Sally (*V/O*)   Jaysus, George, leave him alone.

Justin (*V/O*)   Ah I think they had a fight.

Imelda (*V/O*)   Yeah they did! They had a big row! She got engaged. He's too old for her anyway!

Everyone (*V/O*)   IMELDA!

Sally (*V/O*)   Shut up Imelda.

Robert (*V/O*)   Yeah JUST RELAX!

New track.

Teacher 2 (*V/O*)   Ok, guys, It's our last class before the summer break, everybody say 'Awwww'.

Beat for **Joe** *to say 'Awww' (half-heartedly).*

Teacher 1 (*V/O*)   We can't hear you!

Joe *gives a louder half-hearted 'Awww'.*

Teacher 2 (*V/O*)   So, we just want to thank you so much for coming and let you know that we'll be starting back up again in the autumn.

Teacher 1 (*V/O*)   So don't give up on us!

Teacher 2 (*V/O*)   Keep practising over the summer months. We're actually going away this summer. It's just me and him, on a retreat. Tension.

Teacher 1 (*V/O*)   Sexual tension!

Teacher 2 (*V/O*)   We'll see . . . we'll see . . .

Ok! We want to see you all back next season. We need you!

Teacher 1 (*V/O*)   Ok, a few weeks ago, we worked real hard on the shim sham, so let's get right down to busyness.

Teacher 2 (*V/O*)   Business . . .

Teacher 1 (*V/O*)   Busyness and . . .

Both   give it a go.

Scene Two

The shim sham

(*Song*) *Let me go home whiskey* . . .

Joe *begins dancing the Shim Sham on his own.*

May *enters the room. He doesn't see her. As part of the dance he freezes for eight beats. Then as he begins to dance again, she joins in, slightly behind him.*

In the next freeze:

May   Hey.

Joe   Hey . . .!

The freeze ends and she continues to dance. It takes him a second to realise he is not dancing. He joins in hurriedly to catch up with the step.

On the next freeze.

Joe   Good to see you.

May   Good to see you.

They dance on

When they finish dancing the shim sham 'Only a Paper Moon' comes on.

Scene Three

The fifth social

Bit of an awkward silence.

Joe   Do ya wanna get a drink?

May   Sure.

May *and* **Joe** *start to go as if they are going to leave to get a drink. They stop when they realise that there is nowhere in the immediate vicinity to get a drink. One of them says 'Water?' the other one goes 'Yeah water 'or 'Water's good'. They get their bottles of water from their bags.*

There is a bit of a pantomime of drinking the water. She starts to drink and misses a cheers from him. He abandons it just as she notices it and goes for the cheers. Then she does the same thing as he comes back at her.

They drink deeply. He stops but she continues to drink. So he takes another deep drink. Which makes her take another deep drink. Until eventually they can't avoid having a conversation any longer.

Joe   So . . . emmmmm / . . .

She doesn't want to talk about what happened yet.

May   / Come here, what's been going on here? Sean still counting steps?

Joe   Actually he's a new man! The ladies are queuing up to dance with him.

May   No way!

She might give **Sean** *a thumbs-up. Followed by awkward silence. They look around . . .*

Joe   Noelia went home!

May   Why?!

Joe   Ah, I think she was homesick.

May   Awww.

Joe   The pull of the family.

Pause, they look around again . . .

Poor George is still chasing Sally. And /

Both   she likes to fly solo.

They laugh at their shared joke. Pause. They look around again.

May   Oh, I see Regina's still torturing beginners.

Joe   Actually she's torturing more than beginners. We're an item now.

May (*shocked*)   Are ya serious?

He nods . . . which turns into a . . . 'NO!'

May   What?! Oh very good! (*She tips her hat at him.*) Chapeau, chapeau.

Joe   *Chapeau!* (*He hasn't seen this before, he copies the gesture.*) Very good.

But I'll tell you who *is* going out now.

May   Who?

Joe   Imelda . . . and stinky bins.

May   What?!

Joe   Yeah, the first time she danced with him, she stopped and said – You need a shower. He came back the next week smelling gorgeous!

May (*laughing*)   Wonders will never cease . . .

Another water moment. To avoid having to have any serious discussions, one of them takes another deep drink of water. The other one follows suit.

Joe   Listen, I'm sorry about what I said. The last time you were here. I overstepped the mark. Big time.

Beat.

Particularly about the pan pipes.

Beat.

They're a much maligned instrument.

May   No, you were right. They are shite!

Joe   Oh, that's a pity cos I'm after taking an intensive course in pan pipery in case you ever walked back in here.

Beat.

May   I shouldn't have reacted the way I did. I was so mean, I'm sorry. I think I was just trying to convince myself that I was doing the right thing.

Joe   And you weren't?

May   No. (*Shows him the ringless finger.*) We just didn't love each other enough.

And I think to be honest Simon was relieved when I called it.

Joe   Was he?

May   Yeah . . . Deep down . . . We were both just settling cos it was easy.

Joe   And you prefer something that's difficult?

Music: Little Richard's 'Slipping and Sliding.'

May   No, not difficult . . . Better.

This lands on him. There's a moment.

Will we dance?

As they start to dance the final dance the music swells.

Ends.